BRAVE AND CONFIDENT AGAINST BULLYING

MALAK AHMED NOUR

Copyright © Malak Ahmed Nour 2025
All Rights Reserved.

ISBN
Paperback 979-8-89724-531-4
Hardcase 979-8-89777-355-8

This book has been published with all efforts taken to make the material error-free after the consent of the author. However, the author and the publisher do not assume and hereby disclaim any liability to any party for any loss, damage, or disruption caused by errors or omissions, whether such errors or omissions result from negligence, accident, or any other cause.

While every effort has been made to avoid any mistake or omission, this publication is being sold on the condition and understanding that neither the author nor the publishers or printers would be liable in any manner to any person by reason of any mistake or omission in this publication or for any action taken or omitted to be taken or advice rendered or accepted on the basis of this work. For any defect in printing or binding the publishers will be liable only to replace the defective copy by another copy of this work then available.

Contents

Dedication

I dedicate this book to my family, whose unwavering support and encouragement have been my guiding light. To my parents, who believed in me even when I doubted myself, and to my siblings, who have always been my source of inspiration.

I also dedicate this book to every young dreamer, just like me, who has faced challenges and doubts but continues to push forward with hope and determination. This book is for anyone who believes that their voice matters and that age is no barrier to achieving great things.

Lastly, I dedicate this book to my future self—may you always remember how far you've come, and may you continue to strive for growth, knowledge, and the pursuit of your dreams.

This journey is just beginning, and I hope my words inspire you to keep writing your own story just as I am writing mine.

Preface

This book is a reflection of my very short journey, a story of growth, self-discovery, and the courage to dream big, even at a young age. I never imagined I would be here today, writing a book to share with the world. At just 13 years old, I've come to understand that life isn't about waiting for the perfect moment or the right age to start pursuing your dreams—it's about believing in yourself and taking the first step, no matter how small it may seem.

When I was younger, I faced many challenges that tested my strength and determination. There were times when I doubted myself and questioned my abilities. But through writing, I found a way to express my thoughts and emotions, to channel my dreams and fears into words. It was through writing that I learned how to stand up for myself, how to rise above the negativity and bullying that sometimes surrounded me, and how to embrace my own voice.

This book is not just about my love for writing. It's about how I used writing as a tool for self-development and overcoming obstacles. I wrote my first story at the age of 13, and it was a story about a brave girl named Laila who faced bullying but found the courage to achieve her dreams. As I wrote about Laila, I realised that her story was also my story. Like Laila, I learned that the path to success isn't always smooth, but it's the resilience and determination to keep going that truly matter.

The theme of this book is simple but powerful: you are the architect of your own future. Your dreams are not defined by your age or by the challenges you face. They are defined by your ability to believe in yourself, to overcome obstacles, and to stay true to your vision.

This book is as much for me as it is for anyone who picks it up. It's my way of reminding myself of how far I've come and how much I can achieve in the future. It's my message to others, especially young people, that your voice matters and your dreams are valid. I want to show you that you don't have to wait until you're older or have a perfect plan to start. You can start now.

I hope that through my words, you find the courage to chase your own dreams, never give up, and always believe in the power of your voice. This is just the beginning of my journey, and I can't wait to see where writing takes me next.

Thank you for being a part of this journey with me.

Malak Nour

Muscat, Sultanate of Oman

2025

Chapter 1

About Me

1.1 A Thirteen-Year-Old Writing About a Girl of Sixteen

I was born in 2011 in Sudan, the country I hold dear to my heart. I've been fortunate to grow up surrounded by the love of my family—my father, my mother, and my younger sister, who is four years younger than me. Despite the age difference, we share a special bond, and those four years feel almost non-existent. To me, she is more than just a sister; she's a close friend.

Our lives have always been filled with love, contentment, and care. My parents have worked tirelessly to ensure that my sister and I feel supported, and they extend the same care to our extended family. It's in the environment of love and trust that I've developed into a self-confident person, even at such a young age.

As I grew older and became more aware of the world around me, I began to interact more with others my age—relatives, friends, and neighbours. Yet, there's not much I remember from my early childhood, especially before I turned three. The one memory that stands out, though, is how my parents used to hand me the phone to calm me down when I cried or to keep me entertained. They always said that, just like all the kids my age in the era, I would grow up with a connection to technology.

Looking back now, I realise that my bond with technology began there. The phone became a source of entertainment, joy, and even information. But I always avoided things that made me unhappy or upset. It was simply in my nature—and I think it is true for most children—to seek happiness and steer clear of things that bring sadness.

As I got older, my interest in technology only deepened. I became more adept at using my phone and began exploring the world of technology in new ways. Eventually, I started watching videos on various topics, and some of them were about bullying. At first, I didn't know much about bullying, but soon, I realised that it was something that happened in real life, especially at school. As I watched those videos, I learned the importance of standing up against bullies and how to be brave and confident in such situations.

The lesson became even more meaningful when I started witnessing bullying firsthand at my own school. I quickly understood that no one should ever feel the need to bully others and that it's crucial to have the courage to face bullies with strength. It was during this time that I realised I had developed a skill—the ability to be brave and stand tall in the face of adversity.

When I was 13, I reached a significant milestone: I participated in my first writing competition. I forgot to mention earlier that I absolutely love the English language and, at times, I consider it to be my first language, not Arabic. The competition was held in Muscat, Oman, a country where my family had moved to in 2021. The moment I saw the theme of the competition, I knew it was my chance to write a story about bullying and how to confront it with bravery. Without hesitation, I chose a theme that resonated deeply with me: How can a girl be brave and confident enough to face bullying and achieve her ultimate goals, ultimately learning to be proud of herself first?

I was determined to express my thoughts, and as I wrote, I poured my experiences and feelings into the words. I knew how it felt to face challenges, and the idea of bravery in the face of adversity meant a lot to me. The story I wrote was about strength, self-acceptance, and not letting anything stand in the way of your dreams, no matter what others might say or do.

Writing the story felt liberating. It was more than just a competition; it was an opportunity for me to share something personal, to show that a person can rise above difficulties and find the courage to become the best version of themselves. That experience, my first writing competition, became one of the most important steps in my journey, both as a writer and as someone learning to be proud of who I am.

I named the story "Time's Promise"—a story about a brave girl (Laila) who faced numerous challenges on her journey to becoming a medical doctor and an author. Below, I'll share the details of her journey and how she fought to overcome her obstacles and achieve her dreams.

1.2 Time's Promise

Laila's story is a powerful journey of growth, resilience, and eventual reconciliation with her father. She begins her life struggling with a severe illness that limits her childhood, preventing her from playing with friends and leading a normal life. The emotional distance from her father, a wealthy but neglectful man consumed by her business, leaves her feeling abandoned. He hires Maryam, a kind nanny, who becomes a surrogate mother to Laila. Through Maryam's warmth and support, Laila finds comfort and a dream to become a doctor, a hope she holds onto despite her challenging circumstances.

When Laila's father reacts harshly to her dream and sends her away to a prestigious boarding school, her life takes another difficult turn. At the school, she faces isolation and bullying, but Aliaa, a fellow student, becomes her protector and best friend. Through Aliaa's support, Laila finds strength to stand up for others and push back against bullies. However, tensions at school lead to an emotional breakdown, and Laila collapses from the stress, leading to her hospitalisation. It's revealed that her health condition has worsened, and though her father is not present, Aliaa stays by her side, offering the love and companionship Laila had longed for.

Laila eventually recovers, but her relationship with her father remains strained. When he finally appears after her hospitalisation, Laila's anger and hurt from years of neglect prevent her from embracing him. However, with time, she forgives him, understanding that her own struggles led her to make mistakes. She pursues her dream of becoming a doctor, and 23 years later, she fulfils that dream, sharing her journey with the world in a book that inspires many. Her lifelong friendship with Aliaa continues to be a source of strength.

In a dramatic turn, Laila learns that her father, now elderly and ill, is her patient. The emotional confrontation in the hospital bed brings them closer as her father expresses deep regret for the years he failed her. Laila forgives him, and in a moment of reconciliation, she becomes his surgeon, saving his life. As he recovers, they rebuild their relationship, and Laila begins to feel the closeness she had always wanted. Through her journey, Laila learns the importance of forgiveness, healing, and the deep bond that can form when love and understanding replace old wounds.

The story ends on a note of pride and fulfilment. Laila's dream of becoming a doctor is realised, and her relationship with her father evolves. They both find healing in each other's presence, and Laila finally feels a sense of happiness and closeness with the man who once seemed so distant. Her story is one of personal transformation, showing that while the past cannot be changed, the future holds the possibility for redemption, love, and new beginnings.

1.3 A Step Towards Growth

Although I didn't win my first writing competition (Time's Promise), where competitors from all over Oman participated through their schools, it marked the beginning of something important in my life: a deeper understanding of perseverance. The competition was fierce, and as I looked around at my peers, each one striving to make their mark with their own stories, I couldn't help but feel a little disappointed. I had worked so hard, poured my heart into my writing, and yet, the gold trophy slipped through my fingers.

But there was a lesson in this failure—an important lesson about resilience and the power of persistence. I knew that winning wasn't the only marker of success. The experience, the learning, and the courage to continue after not winning were just as important. I couldn't allow one setback to determine the path I would take.

So, I made a decision. I wouldn't give up. I would write again. And this time, I would strive even harder.

1.4 The Second Chance

I soon found myself participating in another competition, this time within my school. It felt different. This time, I wasn't focused solely on the outcome. I focused on the process, on putting my heart into my work, and on telling a story that mattered to me. The theme for this competition was powerful: A brave man from Palestine protecting his granddaughter from being gunned down.

The story I wrote wasn't just about heroism; it was about love, sacrifice, and the courage to protect what matters most. It reflected strength in the face of overwhelming odds, and it spoke to a universal truth: courage isn't the absence of fear; it is the ability to face fear with the determination to do what is right.

When the results were announced, I was overwhelmed with joy—I won! My story had resonated with the judges, and it was awarded a special prize: a cub-shaped trophy that, though golden, wasn't really about the material value. The trophy, to me, symbolised much more. It wasn't the kind of gold you wear around your neck or display proudly on a shelf. It was a gold of resilience, of overcoming doubt, and of trusting in myself even when the odds were stacked against me.

1.5 The True Meaning of Victory

The cub-shaped trophy I received may not have been gold in the traditional sense, but to me, it held more meaning than any gold medal ever could. It wasn't just about the competition or the award—it was about what I had learned from the journey. I realised that success isn't about achieving everything at once; it's about persistence, self-belief, and staying true to your values even when things don't go according to plan.

Looking back at my journey, I can see that my first failure was essential. It gave me the motivation to push further, to dig deeper, and to challenge myself even more. That failure taught me that the true reward lies in the effort, in the courage to try again, and in the growth that happens along the way.

Winning the second competition, along with the story of Laila, sparked something in me. It encouraged me to complete the full book I had been working on. I wanted to create something that would empower others to face bullying and difficulties in life with strength and resilience. After writing the book, I felt more confident than ever. It wasn't just about winning or proving something to others; it was about sending a message to the bullies that they are wrong. The ones who face bullying are strong, and they can overcome anything they struggle with.

This book I wrote is not just a story I crafted for recognition; it's a message to let people know that life isn't easy when you're bullied. I've faced so many challenges in my life, and I've learned to be strong. I want others to understand that they too should never give up, no matter how hard things get. You have to show the world that you can face your bullies head-on. I did that before, and after it, I felt like I became brave and confident, for the first time, standing up to those who tried to break me.

And the message is for everyone, especially those my age: Don't let anyone make you feel small. Life will throw challenges your way, but you are capable of overcoming them. You are stronger than you think. Let the bullies know your next move because they have no power over you.

Chapter 2

Bullying

2.1 Self Searching

I share my personal journey of dealing with bullying, both as a child and as someone who has come to understand its deeper emotional and psychological impact. The intention here is not to lecture but to reflect on my experiences and offer insights to others facing similar challenges. I believe that through sharing my story and the lessons I've learned, I can shed light on a painful yet important topic, turning my experiences into something that might help someone else navigate their own struggles with bullying.

2.2 Bullying in Depth

When I first encountered bullying, I didn't fully grasp the weight of the term. It was a word I had heard but never truly understood until I became the victim. The harm caused wasn't always physical, but the cruelty of words, actions, and attitudes left scars on my soul that were far deeper. There were moments where I felt like I wanted to retaliate, perhaps with violence, to defend myself. But over time, I realised that violence only escalates the situation. Reacting with anger or aggression may seem like an immediate solution, but it doesn't address the root of the problem.

My perspective on bullying evolved when I moved to Muscat, a city rich in cultural diversity, and started attending a school with students from various backgrounds. It was there that I witnessed bullying in its many forms: verbal abuse, exclusion, and even physical intimidation. This prompted me to do more research to understand the behaviour behind bullying. I reached out to others, engaged in conversations, and even reflected on the teachings of my religion, Islam, which emphasises kindness and respect. I realised that bullying is more than just harmful—it is a profound form of disrespect, violating the values of empathy, compassion, and dignity.

Through my research, I learned that bullying is often a repeated behaviour that involves one person exerting power or control over another. It isn't always a one-time event but something that can manifest in various forms, including:

Physical Bullying: Hitting, pushing, or damaging someone's belongings.

Verbal Bullying: Name-calling, insults, threats, and harsh words meant to hurt.

Social/Relational Bullying: Excluding others, spreading rumours, or manipulating relationships.

Cyberbullying: Using online platforms to harass, threaten, or humiliate someone.

Each type of bullying can have lasting effects on the person being targeted, leading to emotional pain, anxiety, depression, and a profound sense of isolation. It doesn't just affect one's mental health—it can impact academic performance, social interactions, and even physical health.

To combat bullying, we need to foster environments of empathy, respect, and understanding. It is essential for schools and communities to ensure that bullying is reported, addressed quickly, and that both the victims and the bullies receive the help they need. The bullies, too, may be grappling with their own unresolved issues. Support is necessary for both sides to create an environment where bullying is not tolerated.

2.3 Children and Bullying

As a child, I was deeply shocked when I first witnessed bullying. The cruelty of it was jarring, and it felt fundamentally unfair. It was hard to understand why anyone would hurt another person, especially for reasons that seemed trivial, like appearance or socioeconomic background. Some children were bullied for not having the latest fashion or gadgets, while others were targeted simply because they didn't fit into a particular mould.

The emotional toll bullying takes on victims is not always visible. It's not just about the words that are said; it's about the pain they leave behind. Children are often ill-equipped to handle these situations, and the lack of coping mechanisms can lead to feelings of frustration, sadness, and powerlessness.

Through my experiences, I learned that bullying often stems from fear or insecurity in the bully and that the victims are not at fault. The emotional scars can linger, and the damage is not easily undone. The lesson I took away was the importance of responding to bullying with empathy, both for those being hurt and for those who may be doing the hurting. Understanding the pain behind the actions can make all the difference in how we address and prevent bullying.

2.4 What Bullying Leaves Behind

The aftermath of bullying is not just about the immediate hurt; it's about the long-term effects. The scars left behind often remain long after the event itself. For me, memories of being bullied conjure up feelings of isolation, shame, and a sense of powerlessness. My self-esteem took a serious hit, and I often replayed the moments of humiliation in my mind. In one instance, I tried to confront my bullies with anger, but they only made things worse. The situation escalated, leading to a deeper sense of conflict and emotional turmoil.

The experience taught me an important lesson: responding with anger doesn't solve the problem. The best way to confront bullying is not through retaliation, but with calmness, confidence, and assertiveness. Standing up to bullies doesn't mean being aggressive; it means having the courage to rise above their negativity and not letting their words or actions define you.

2.5 Strong but Not Tough

I remember the overwhelming anger I felt when I was bullied. Every fibre of my being wanted to fight back, to defend myself in any way I could. But deep down, I knew that it wouldn't solve anything—it would only escalate the conflict and likely get me into trouble. I realised that true strength doesn't lie in physical retaliation; it lies in emotional control, patience, and choosing kindness over conflict.

Many people say that bullying "toughens" children, but the idea is misleading. The reality is that bullying leaves lasting emotional and physical consequences. It's not about being "tough" or becoming hardened to the pain. The real strength comes from building resilience, developing inner strength, and having the confidence to face adversity without letting it dictate who you are.

In the end, I learned that I don't need to be tough or mean to stand up for myself. True strength lies in maintaining my dignity and staying grounded in my beliefs. It's about being confident in who I am, remaining calm under pressure, and treating others with the respect and kindness they deserve, no matter how they treat me. By doing so, I've learned to face bullying with the courage and confidence I once lacked. And my hope is that others who read there will find the strength to do the same.

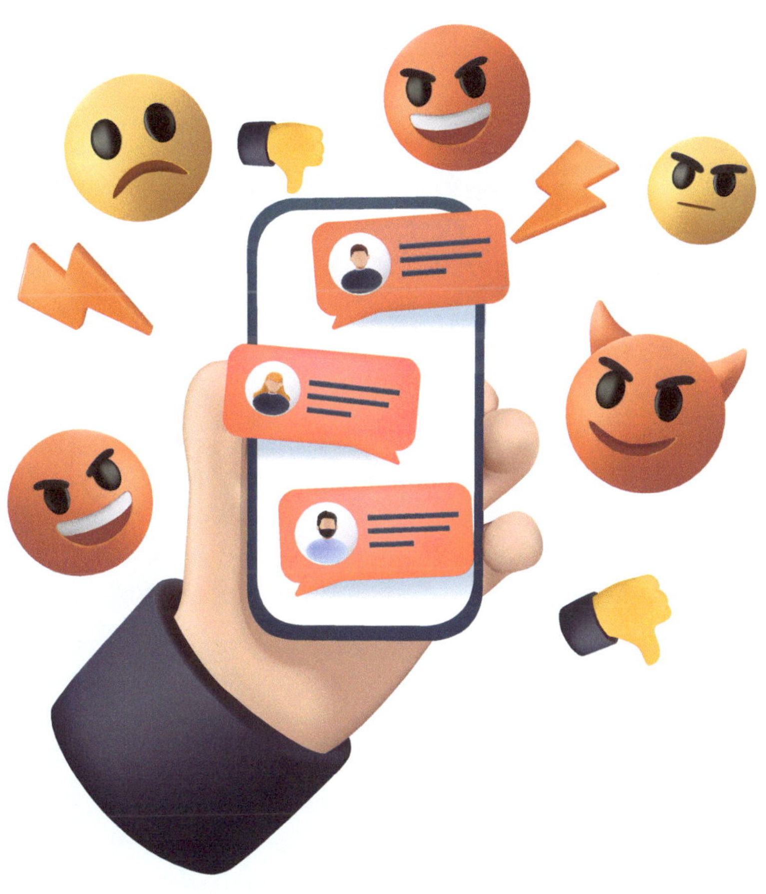

Chapter 3

Bullying in the Media

I want to delve deeper into how bullying transcends the physical boundaries of schools and homes. Through the stories and reflections shared here, I aim to encourage a greater understanding of the role that both home and school play in shaping who we are and how we deal with challenges like bullying. Just like the fictional story of Laila, whose journey in a media-filled world shaped her resilience, our own experiences within these spaces contribute to our growth, strength, and perspective. By reflecting on these stories, I want to show readers how we can deal with bullying, grow stronger, and create positive spaces for everyone.

3.1 Laila's Places

While Laila's story is fictional, it has remained with me as a way of understanding bullying's impact on our lives. The places Laila encountered hardships—those "Media" spaces—are more than just physical locations; they are the settings in which our personalities are formed and tested. Like Laila, we all encounter moments of weakness and strength in our own lives that help define who we are. The experiences we go through in places like our homes and schools can build us up or break us down, depending on how we handle them.

In Laila's world, the "Media" represents the environments where we learn, struggle, and sometimes fail. For many of us, these environments are schools and homes, the places we spend the most time. The challenges we face there, including bullying, are part of a bigger picture—one that ultimately shapes our future selves.

3.2 Homes and Schools as Second Homes

We all know the difference between home and school, but what exactly makes these spaces so different? To illustrate the contrast, I want to share a personal story:

In first grade, I loved hanging out with my friends. I was eager to visit their homes, just like they visited mine. However, my parents were reluctant to let me go, and I couldn't understand why. I felt left out and frustrated, especially when my friends' families allowed them to visit. My family noticed my unhappiness and took the time to explain their concerns. They explained that home was the safest place for me, where I could feel protected and loved.

Slowly, I began to understand. I spent more time with my family, and we enjoyed simple, fun activities like playing board games or watching movies together. Through this, I realised that home is more than just a place to live—it's a "safe" home, where

I can truly be myself, surrounded by love and support. It is where I can rest and feel accepted.

The experience helped me grasp the concept that home isn't just a physical space; it's an environment where I feel valued and safe. And that's what makes it my second "safe" home. In contrast, school is where we are exposed to a wide range of experiences—some positive, but others, like bullying, can test our limits and make us feel vulnerable.

3.3 Schools Are Full of Bullies

We all know that schools can sometimes feel like battlegrounds—places where we learn, grow, but also face challenges, including bullying. But why does bullying happen in schools, and how does it affect us? Let me share an experience from my own life to explain:

In sixth grade, I joined an international school in Oman, and for the first time, I had boys in my class. At first, they seemed a bit annoying, but I soon realised that some of them went beyond mere teasing – they started bullying younger students, especially third graders. They targeted the innocent ones, and I hated being in that class.

One day, I found myself sitting alone at lunch, as my friends had to leave for a project. The boys approached me and asked why I was sitting by myself. I didn't respond, and they just walked away. They kept trying to mess with me, but I chose to ignore them, which only seemed to frustrate them even more.

As I stayed calm and didn't react to their taunts, I noticed their plans to get under my skin were failing. Eventually, one of the boys admitted, "We tried our best to make you uncomfortable, but you didn't let it affect you." Despite their insults, I didn't care. One of the teachers saw the situation, and the bullies ran off. I decided to report the incident to the head of the primary school. Although the bullies didn't seem remorseful, they stopped bothering me after that.

The experience taught me a vital lesson: bullies may try to hurt you, but how you respond determines how much power they have over you. Staying calm and not letting their actions affect your emotions is one way to take control of the situation.

(You Never Judge a Book by Its Cover)

3.4 The Enemies

Throughout my life, I encountered bullies. These individuals became what I initially perceived as enemies—barriers to my peace, happiness, and sense of self-worth. But over time, I realised that they were not real enemies; instead, they were the reflections of my inner struggles, fears, and doubts. They were like mirrors, showing me where I needed to grow. This book is my journey of shifting my perspective and seeing bullies not as obstacles to my happiness, but as stepping stones that helped me become stronger, more confident, and more resilient.

Here, I'll share how I learned to deal with bullies, how I learned to use their negativity as fuel for my personal growth, and how you can too. The truth is, bullies can only become true enemies if you allow them to control your narrative. By taking control of your own story, you can turn these moments of challenge into opportunities for empowerment.

I remember the first time I was bullied. The sting of harsh words, the feeling of being different or unwanted, and the loneliness that followed were overwhelming. It felt like an attack, and I reacted the way many people do—by withdrawing, by feeling sorry for myself, and by letting it affect my confidence. Bullies seemed like powerful forces that could destroy my peace, and I let them have that power.

But this was just the beginning of a process—a long journey of self-discovery. Over time, I started to notice something: each instance of bullying became a point of reflection, a moment where I could either shrink and hide or rise and confront. I soon realised that I had a choice.

It was a turning point when I realised that bullies, instead of being obstacles, could serve as catalysts for my personal growth. Instead of focusing on their words or actions, I began to focus on what they were teaching me about myself.

Bullies can trigger a lot of internal challenges—insecurities, fears, and doubts. But these emotional responses are not the enemy; they are invitations for me to face those fears, challenge them, and overcome them. When I saw bullies as reflections of the parts of myself I still needed to work on, they stopped being my enemies. Instead, they became mirrors, showing me where I needed to grow stronger.

Chapter 4

Brave, Confident, and Bullying

4.1 Laila's Confidence

In imagining the story of Laila, I can feel the weight of her journey. Her path wasn't easy, and it mirrors the challenges many of us face. Laila found herself caught in the struggle between her true self and the pressures of a world that constantly told her she wasn't enough. Like the media's portrayal of perfection, bullying reflected the harshest expectations. She was faced with a choice: conform to the standards that society pushed on her, or take the path of self-acceptance and defy the voices that sought to tear her down. Over time, Laila found the strength to make that choice. She realised that her uniqueness was her power—something that could never be taken away.

In my own life, I have often thought about how much Laila's story parallels my own experiences. Growing up, I also struggled with the weight of expectations—expectations about how I should look, behave, or fit in with the crowd. It was easy to feel like I wasn't measuring up, like I had to hide parts of myself to avoid judgement or rejection. There were times when I questioned whether I was enough, if I was doing enough to belong, or if something was wrong with me. But as I grew older, I started to realise that the path to confidence and bravery wasn't about pretending to be someone I wasn't. It was about learning to embrace the parts of me that made me different, just like Laila did.

I imagined that if I were in Laila's shoes, I might have struggled with those same fears—the fear of not fitting in, the fear of being called out or made to feel small. But I also understood that strength lies not in hiding but in facing those fears. There were times when I, too, tried to fit into a mould that didn't represent who I was. I thought that changing parts of myself would make things easier, would make me less of a target. But the more I tried to hide, the more I felt disconnected—not just from others, but from my true self. It was an exhausting game of pretending.

What I've come to realise, just like Laila, is that my true strength comes from being authentic. Pretending to be someone I'm not would only lead to feelings of isolation, and in the end, it would hurt the relationships I had with the people who mattered most. And so, my journey has been about learning to face the fear head-on, to stand tall in my own skin, and to show up as my real self—both at school and at home. I want to be the same person in both places, embracing who I am, even when it feels difficult.

Sometimes, it feels like the world is pushing against me, trying to shape me into something I'm not. But what I've learned is that real bravery is about facing those moments and saying,

"This is who I am, and I'm enough." It doesn't mean that I won't feel fear or pain along the way, but that I can rise above it. Like Laila, who found her inner strength through the love and support of those around her, I've learned that I can build my resilience through the connections I make, the people who understand me, and the courage I find within myself.

Creating that courage isn't always easy. There were times when I felt that hiding my true self was the only way to survive bullying. But the more I reflected on it, the more I realised that surviving wasn't enough. I wanted to thrive. And thriving meant staying true to myself, even when it felt like the world wanted me to be someone else. Like Laila, I started to understand that I didn't need to change my behaviour to fit in; I needed to change my mindset—to embrace my uniqueness and face challenges with confidence.

What I've learned is that it's not just about personal strength; it's about creating a community that embraces acceptance, understanding, and kindness. It's about helping others see that bullying doesn't define who we are. By staying authentic, by showing up as our true selves, we create an environment where people feel seen, heard, and valued. And if we all work together, we can create spaces—both at home and at school—where bullying has no place.

In my journey, I've realised that bravery is not the absence of fear. It's the act of feeling fear, acknowledging it, and then stepping forward anyway. Just like Laila, I now understand that each step I take, no matter how small, is a victory over the doubts and fears that once held me back. And with each victory, I become a stronger version of myself—one who is unafraid to embrace individuality and champion others to do the same. Through the process, I hope to inspire not only myself but others to rise above bullying and create a world where we all feel confident, valued, and accepted.

4.2 Personal Growth and Development

Your reflection on self-development and the importance of taking ownership of your journey is deeply empowering. Indeed, self-development begins with you, and the decisions you make today lay the foundation for the future you will create. By reflecting on your experiences, challenges, and aspirations, you gain the clarity and confidence needed to steer your life in the right direction, taking active control of your personal growth.

My imagination of Laila's story of resilience and overcoming obstacles serves as a powerful reminder that challenges are inevitable, but how we face and rise above them is what defines us. Each difficulty, setback, and challenge strengthens your character and resilience. It builds the foundation for future success and helps you move closer to realising your dreams.

As you think about your career, remember that it is more than just a job. Your career is a reflection of your values, passions, and growth. It represents the journey you're on—your persistence, your alignment with what matters most to you, and your ability to adapt to challenges. When you remain true to your values and focus on fulfilling work that aligns with your passion, your career will give you purpose and sustain you through tough times.

External challenges, like bullying or negative experiences, can certainly shake your confidence. However, as you pointed out, these moments offer a unique opportunity to tap into your inner strength and resilience. While it's easy to let others' opinions impact your self-worth, true growth comes from nurturing self-belief and surrounding yourself with supportive people who help you rise above negativity. By remaining resilient and focused on your long-term vision, you can minimise the impact of external pressures on your sense of self.

Self-development is a continuous journey of reflection, learning, and growth. The more you understand your passions, your motivations, and the areas where you can improve, the clearer your path becomes. Your career, just like your personal growth, evolves as you develop new skills and insights. Each challenge is a stepping stone, helping you grow stronger and closer to your goals. Embrace these opportunities and know that, by doing so, you will not only inspire yourself but also inspire those around you.

At the core of this is the fact that you are the architect of your future. Every step you take towards your goals contributes to a life filled with purpose, success, and fulfilment. Your career, self-development, and personal growth are interconnected, and the choices you make today shape the life you lead tomorrow.

Surrounding yourself with trusted individuals who support your vision can speed up the process of achieving your goals. Collaboration and mutual encouragement create momentum that propels you forward. By staying true to your vision and consistently reflecting on your progress, you keep yourself on the path to success.

It's also important to recognise the relationship between career and financial stability. While passion is a driving force, the ability to earn a living allows you the freedom to explore your creativity and fully commit to your professional aspirations. Striking the balance between passion and financial security is crucial. By being honest with yourself about your goals and the realities of the world, you can make decisions that allow you to pursue what excites you while also ensuring financial stability.

Your advice to take initiative and shape your future now is especially valuable. Don't wait for external circumstances or institutions to define your path. Every step you take now lays the groundwork for your future, opening doors for creativity and personal growth. By actively shaping your career and self-development, you are positioning yourself for long-term success.

The journey to your goals is just as important as the destination. Focus on the process, stay true to your vision, and trust in your ability to achieve your dreams with persistence, self-belief, and resilience. And as you reach this point, you will notice that by focusing on your personal growth and self-development, you have pulled yourself out of the "bullying zone". You no longer feel the weight of external negativity as you have strengthened your own belief in yourself. This is the true power of self-development—the ability to build a strong internal foundation that makes the negative behaviour of others irrelevant.

By focusing on self-empowerment and growth, you will move beyond the influence of bullying and negative behaviour, finding the strength to focus on your future, your goals, and the positive impact you can have. Feel that shift within yourself and start making your plans—the journey towards your better self has already begun.

The practical outcomes of self-development offer powerful deliverables to bullies by transforming you into a resilient, confident individual who is no longer easily affected by their behaviour. As you continue to grow and evolve, your internal strength, emotional resilience, and commitment to your goals become your greatest defences. By consistently embodying self-worth, setting boundaries, and pursuing your passions, you show that bullies cannot control your narrative or your future.

Self-development is the ultimate form of anti-bullying, as it allows you to not only protect yourself from the harm of others' negativity but also grow stronger through each challenge. The more you invest in your growth, the more you empower yourself to rise above bullying, achieving your dreams with integrity, focus, and grace.

Chapter 5

Dream It Possible

At the age of 13, many young people are still figuring out who they want to be, what they want to do, and what their life's purpose will be. For me, that journey began with a single decision: to write. I didn't know then that writing would become my passion, my voice, and ultimately, my path to self-discovery.

When I first encountered the story of Laila, I didn't know that her journey would have a profound impact on mine. Laila was a young girl, much like me, who faced obstacles on her journey towards becoming a medical doctor. She lived with determination, resilience, and a belief in herself that fuelled her every step. But while her path took her through university and medical school, mine took a different route—through the pages of books, the keyboard, and the stories I would share with the world.

Laila's story inspired me to pursue my own dreams, not by following a conventional path, but by crafting my own destiny through writing. While she would become a doctor at 23, I found my purpose as an author at the same age. Through the words I put on paper, I realised that true self-development is not just about the career you build, but about the strength and wisdom you cultivate from within.

5.1 A Life in Words

The first writing competition I entered was in Muscat, Oman. I was just 13. The theme of the competition—about bullying and bravery—struck a chord with me. I knew exactly what I wanted to say: A girl brave enough to face the hardest challenges, to confront the negativity in her life, and to stand tall in the face of adversity. I poured my heart into that story, though I didn't win.

But the failure didn't defeat me. Instead, it propelled me forward. I realised that it wasn't the competition that mattered most; it was the act of writing, of giving voice to the things I deeply felt. The more I wrote, the more I learned about myself. Writing became my method of self-expression, a way to process my experiences and an avenue to shape the world I wanted to create for myself.

5.2 Breaking Free from Expectations

One of the biggest lessons I learned was that success doesn't always come in the form of a degree or a traditional career. In a world where success is often defined by the job title you hold; I began to question why achievements were so tightly linked to career paths. I realised that my journey was not limited to becoming a doctor, lawyer, or engineer. My path could be defined by the words I shared with the world and the impact I made through them.

At 13, I set out to become an author. I didn't wait for validation. I didn't wait for someone to tell me I was good enough. Instead, I began writing my story, sharing my experiences, and hoping that my words would inspire others to follow their own passions.

5.3 The Power of Anti-Bullying and Self-Belief

Throughout my life, I've dealt with bullies—people who tried to diminish my worth and derail my ambitions. But something powerful happened over time. I didn't just learn how to ignore the bullies. I began to understand their behaviour and how to stand strong against it. I realised that it wasn't just bullying I was up against—it was a mindset. A mindset that dictated that others should belittle you in order to feel powerful. But I rejected that mindset. I knew I was capable of more.

With every word I wrote, I created a shield for myself. A shield made not of anger, but of self-belief. I refused to let the negativity of others define me. I built resilience, focus, and determination, using every criticism as fuel to prove to myself that I was worthy of my dreams.

5.4 My Own Path

At 23, Laila reached her dream of becoming a doctor. But my dream came to life earlier. I became an author at 13. My words travelled across the world, inspiring those who read them to believe in themselves, to chase their dreams, and to never let anyone diminish their worth.

Writing is my calling. It has always been my tool for self-development and growth. While Laila's path to becoming a doctor was a part of her journey, mine was about finding my voice and learning to use it. The greatest achievement in my life isn't defined by the career I hold but by the impact I can make with my words.

In the chapters of this book, I want to share not just Laila's story, but my own. I want to remind myself—and others—of the importance of resilience, self-belief, and the courage to pursue our dreams, even when the path seems unconventional.

5.5 The Power of Writing and Inspiration

I wrote this book not only for others but also for myself. This journey has been as much about me as it is about the world I want to reach. I'm proud of the writer I've become, and I'm proud of the journey I'm on. By sharing my story, I hope to inspire others my age to believe in their potential, to reject the negativity that surrounds them, and to always strive to be the best version of themselves.

This book is a testament to the power of self-development, resilience, and the importance of staying true to one's goals, no matter how unconventional they may seem. Whether you're pursuing a career in medicine, art, or writing, your journey is yours alone. And you have the power to make it whatever you want it to be.

5.6 My Message

As I sit here, writing these words, I realise how far I've come. The journey from a young girl with dreams of becoming an author to a 13-year-old who now shares her words with the world has been an incredible one. And as I continue to grow, I know that my story is far from over.

So, to anyone who reads these pages: Your dreams are valid. Your voice matters. Don't let anyone tell you otherwise. The power of self-development, self-belief, and resilience is within you. And if I, at the age of 13, can publish this book, so can you.

You are your greatest asset. Trust in your potential, follow your passion, and create the future you deserve.

The End

www.ingramcontent.com/pod-product-compliance
Lightning Source LLC
Chambersburg PA
CBHW040916110726
48005CB00006B/914